MW01226040

FAKE MATH

ryan fitzpatrick

FAKE MATH

ryan fitzpatrick

SNARE BOOKS . MONTREAL

Edited by Jason Christie and Jon Paul Fiorentino
Designed by Jon Paul Fiorentino
Copyedited by Mike Spry
Typeset in Gill Sans and Minion

LIBRARY AND ARCHIVES CANADA CATALOGUING IN PUBLICATION

Fitzpatrick, Ryan, 1978-
        Fake math / Ryan Fitzpatrick.

Poems.
ISBN 978-0-9739438-5-6

        I. Title.

PS8611.I893F35 2007   C811'.6   C2007-905309-2

Printed and bound in Canada

Represented in Canada by the Literary Press Group
Ditributed by LitDistCo

SNARE BOOKS
4302 St. Urbain Street #1A
Montreal QC
H2W 1V5
snarebooks.wordpress.com

Canada Council   Conseil des Arts
for the Arts   du Canada

Snare Books gratefully acknowledges the financial support of the Canada Council for the Arts.

"Moments are the elements of profit."

Karl Marx, Capital Vol. 1

THE DENATURED POEM

The most ambitious
tipping bottle is status
and power based.

That Archimedes could lift
position in a love poem
slavery, trade unions, at all.

The poor, yet educated,
structurally sound, watch
very big people get paid.

A couple of bottles and
the city relaxes, forgets
public reports and meetings.

After a star fuses, will it
tolerate ambiguity, make
realities concrete?

A totemic court crafts
small holes in hominid
static complexity.

That Euclid is a denatured
denizen; geometric
sounds left heartbreaking.

To recollect a life –
swooning photographs –
boil off photographs.

In propriety, a warm dish,
ceiling repairs holes blink
in dignity or rain.

A useful window on
the state building trusts, or
consumer model makes good.

That a poet may wish
to play at memorabilia
stirred by explosions.

If mathematically true, truth
creaking wheels move
statutes in clear relationships.

THIS POETRY SEEMS LIKE A GOOD RACKET

First off, my poem forgot how
peanut butter and jam tastes.
In kindergarten, a strong coffee
soap opera, my poem caught a fish.

Like a spoilt child, my budgie died.
Got kid deep in this dimlyness. Fog
of cadence a frog prince seems to like.
Shoot up the sky, a chirpy lullaby.

From true fireworks, rue voice soon burst.
Spare thee quarters when Klein takes
jobs in the junk. A jelly scansion drops
to the floor, a sack of strong coffee.

PLEASE SIR, I WANT SOME MORE

Dear Socialism, prohibition makes me
cry into my beer. O Socialism, let loose
your icy stares as here nor there swings
open like old-fashioned musicals; sing song
social experimentation tiptoes into pubs.

For each pulse returned a volley, complete
with leather seats, made by back-packed tweens
charge from a caf table toward the master,
basin and spoon in hand saying a marketing trick
forms a sort of thick, caustic liquid.

Fair Socialism, dispense with the seatbelt
and encourage the Doppler surge of Ford
ladling cheap gasoline into my eyes.
I would like some hate mail, please,
letter bombs, molotov cocktails, spam.

THE METAPHORIST

A window overlooks a bank of ATM's.
A convenience store with gas. Baristas;
alphabets. These galleries begin
as poems. In a craft economy, paint
tender, not tenderly. With scissors,
orange fonts collage lotto tickets.

Down the hall, the restrooms need flowers
with stems hugging photos. A fine cut
from painted wood. A gasoline generator
cut from vending machines. Surely,
art is about craft. An audience senses
jet models careening woolen in composition.
Yet when the heart gets looped, art
gets the hangman's noose. Two weavers
as good as a metaphorist. A loose fitting.

Love as cardboard; luck as budget.
Metonymy as rent; metaphor as
pulse. A base as posterboard;
ideology as glitter. Pencils as erasers;
trees as end table manufacture.

A bear and balloon help bees sell honey.
Fuck alters global climate. A sharp knife
flattens out any wrinkles. Ostranenie spins
a cultural demand dizzy. Breathing seeks
hiccups. Streamflow re-enacts civil war.
Cannons canonized with plaques as
historical monuments. A self-involved forest.

When the heart is involved, poetry
is an open-ended envelope, glue side up.
Just before the canoe hits the paddle,
the water paddles itself.

A SHINING BEACON

On brilliance: a filled cup –
a hilly cup; rhyme glances
green; poet oversees hats and
skirts; nails, lumbar, capital.

On insight: eureking; sovereign
tee; freedom – cheap as free; idea –
ideology pancakes asphalt; power
grid – peeing; parakeets – parrots.

On craft: a belt-sander; sand
in my panties; pearl in my urn –
earn, earn; social capital – surfing
horse; throat rainbow, catch asshole.

CAREERISM AND THE CARNIVALIST IMPULSE

Gimmick after gimmick! Branding
dialogues with careening egoism.

Obedience after idiosyncracy! Bad art
barks lip-sync urban anxiety.

Polyphony after prodigy! Survivalism
perpetuates moral humping.

Answerability after expediency! Expense
contrasts geology with rock and roll.

Solemnity after conflict! Success
records noise after civic celebrity.

A LIFE LESS ORIGINARY

Dear Spongebob, how can I make
a life from non-sequiturs? My eyes
burn books with knives and jobs
hierarch steak to stake to stake.

A wizard; a woozle. Under the bed;
under the booze. Make sense; make
densely overpopulated. State sentence;
state legislature. Bed rest; dead.

I'm afraid. I connect wires to
turbines. I spin in place. I light
fires in sense. I plagiarize openly.
I eat meat. I watch the clock.

THE NEW POEM

A poem in here
lights a quite dark text
with electrons, or
a pain in my head
from ADHD. A caffeine
typo, or sentence feels
under the whether.
I could eat some words, or
a cinnamon danish.
Focus still light on
a desk lamp, or
birds tap on my window
twittering showtunes
so I lose pupils which
shrink, or Freud.
A poem with
material superstition,
or dirty laundry (detergent, or
determinant). A poem
with box art, or botox, or
tax alert specialists.
So close poem wins
by a fare, or brew time.
Poem is new, or
never. Answer is longer
lines, or pining (love note, or
hip graphic) (reference self, or
reference pelvis).
A poem for Elvis, or a baby
seal. A club for beating
back organizational

pub nights, or flipper your
checkmark up the left ramp.
Circle the right on, or
deviate, but in a funtime way.
The heart spins plates, or is in
the broom closet with
a vacuum love of a lifetime,
or HBO. It's a burn, or
a pain. Elbow hits shag
carpet, or a poem bleeds
all over the Pine-solled
lino. A messy shit, or
tsk tsk. Empire is all clear
with a healthy glow, or
dams up flow. But gophers
keep digging holes and the
horse keeps needing splints, or
damn, why did you forget
the ointment? I am sad
when shelves empty, dude, or
a pulp headache. Wait,
it's an option I want
to bubble up to, or
an American Idol, or
nail polish. A poem is
a design innovation,
or toke on reefer (a stigma,
or a cigarette, or
a signification, or a
triple word score). A potential
conflict, or a dysfunctional
new poem. A soapy line,
or a loamy stanza.

An Aspirin has a
compositional rigour, or stop
discovering stuff, would you?

ON STAKING A CLAIM

Hand me the money, chump. Bump
mining last. Consider maps drawn.
Competition! Claim Jump Law
gets a brake shoe to the face.

Labeling disputes at birth. Start with
feasibility, or feast on chocolate. Do
both! Negotiate a tree, or free federal
codes. The Yukon, or I own you.

Every chiropractor loves lordship. Claim
a meteor broke your poor, poor back.
Leather jacket supplies pickaxe and
toughness. Mine. Mine, mine, mine.

WHY DO YOU KEEP SECOND GUESSING YOURSELF?

You've been Maxorzed! Now, do the math!
Do you "self-reflect" or "self-ruminant"?
Figure out which way makes you blow
chunks into inspirational keepsakes.

For your love, I keep crawling down
into keystone cops: slapstick beach season.
The swoosh says "Just Do It" so let's fuck
if your boyfriend likes another girl.

The city's a chocolate chip cookie
once you've submitted your rank order, so
why bring up Snoop Dogg? Your "Mr. Wrong"
experiences are just a computer algorithm!

THAT'S SO HIGH SCHOOL

Dear Bigg Snoop Dogg, let's reconsider
your archaic views of feminism. That's so gay
is typical teen jargon in some schools.

Maybe while Bayside High lived in
the Pacific Paliisades took up with that
little tart that so gay is stupid and weird.

When her high school classmates say,
"That's so illegit!" Raven Symone answers
"That's so f-ing GAY! Or is it?"

Most professional trucking schools have
classes on pimp-slapping hoes. Although,
teachers patrol the halls looking for gay activity.

Find out about that gay Disney girls tune
singing homophobia rocks. Surely Snoop,
women would rather be bikinied than respected.

OWNERSHIP POLICIES

They should get a liquor store and
practice robberies. Or maybe push
gayness to stop the white race.

Women are not in the kitchen anymore
and I, for one, am hungry for
change. As a man, I am unable to.

We could own the market with slurs.
Only rich, white men pay for cable,
and the gays are too busy to watch.

Robots would turn the cranks, but
they are too expensive. People are
more cost effective and argue less.

SOCIAL COMMODITIES

If a pen mark stays gold.
If a word is a foodstamp, then good.
Value treadmill early in herd.
Hoard out money which miracles.
No single out any circulation.
Worldview has turned.
Just because we screw doesn't mean.
Just because we assume swoosh pants.
Tradition and the tattooed cerebellum.
Sweat and swoon of commodity fetishism.
Totemic icon of commodity, and test drive.
Art is a dirty word.
A heart of purina.
In the sun on the beach.
Loving the V8's hum.
Bud of calm, blossom of hysteria.
Why gold confronts the linen as money.
Turns the neutral "truck" to "bird".
A Mastercard look-alike.
Fun like a smutifier.
Puppies tell kids truth.
Find out you belong fabricating.
Swipes the infrared wink.
Textbook perfect in the cockpit.
A new magic system.
Clauses instead of chiro laws.
What's so wrong with upstanding?
To a sharp point: Hilary Duff; the internet.
Onward upward mobility.
Art is a hardwood tree.
Harry Potter and the Abuse of Underage Wizardry.

Fields pine for Gap jeans, low rise preferably.
Heart is hot lava, disco dancing, Barbie.
A custom, super-magnum vend-o-mat.
Up my skirt promotes circulation.
Poems like platform shoes.
"Yuck Factor": an obstacle.
A pen and pencil set (65 cents).
A pill to deal with debts.
Crude repression makes for blow-out.
A spot on Freud's "Hot Sexual Obscenity."
Intelligent at one time and gasp.
Crowbar puncture credit card.
Public airwaves just sand and ocean.
If you wanna act industrious.
Chiropractic all you want.
Fucking wack is static.
Patented In-Seatro Technology.
Plot floor mounts political correctness.
Eats up the sexual fetishization, mmm.
Escape from the forest map tattooed in brain.
Salmon pitches glacial beer.
A violence continually reorganized and sold.
Bold in eyecatching brand.
Cows end up in the cutting room.
Picture face assumes cartoon role.
Nevertheless seems Milton Friedman.
Puppies are a crucial alphabet.
Art gives bunnies bad breath.
Vomit and scabs and gunshot wounds.
Meaty face redneck Popeye.
Black eyes and a rich plot.
A satellite-dish ejaculatorium.
Into a hired mouthpiece.

On a poetics of knee-deep shit.
Shiftwork as leisure behaviour.
Pats the child into civil rule.
Some fine, hand-crafted nerve pain.
Nursing a goal-oriented stain.
Relationship between catalogue and college.
Between census and collage.
To the postmodernist petting zoo.
Loose in a classroom of schoolkids.
Ronald Reagan as the Tooth Fairy.
Fisher-Price heart print thigh high.
Playskool weight belt and inflatable rabid dog.
This Miata turned me racist!
An innocent needlepoint picture.
X-Rays, rainbows, and DVD's.
Capital a poem, sell for profit.
Suture to antique symbol.
Tribalism intense in the shower.
Wade through textual obstacle.
Wonderful cerebro-spinal analgesic.
Much more alarmist panic message.
Biggest kaboom for the buck.
Dear Cliffside Buddhas, all I got was want is this stupid T-Shirt.
Like when Kramer sold Jerry's car for magic beans.
How a rind is a terrible thing to taste.
Wring all sugar from.
Grover eats the bullet raw.
Communiqué a blank wall.
Moralism a bicep anchor.
Hemingway slugs ruby port after hem haw.
Large or crooked roots.
Documentary under the bed.
Why Nader won't do snorkel scenes.

Ocean beach sex fucking sand.
Front of the sentence is the world thong capital.
Cows mount world depression party.
Down the spine and to the organ.
Words and their orphanages.
Supersize my art, please.
Poof, or a lower backache.
Two pages into the epidemic.
To the Queen's credit, skinrash.
Made homogenous and global village.
White on the face and white.
Facecream and other barbed wire.
Chinese superstar or indian maiden.
Trudeau or Mulroney: choose!
Only a question of a messy public.
Pause with an oxford comma.
U.S. Military constructs indestructible sandwich.
Great line up for this year's civil-rights activism.
Visitors can leave their potlatch in the upstairs bedroom.
Frivolously cut jackets with holeable bolshevism.
Mom saturates inflatable chairs.
Zoloft your Bobby Sherman.
Stalin and his crystal meth.
Galactaphonic hot under the candy floss machine.
Tea burns the roof of your house.
Ugly graphemes reject numerous rejections.
Wack images onto thrift store refuse.
Phonemes soldered in white gold.
A leftist politic as cool as a terminator romp.
Sound left in the cutting room.
Icon of new subcultural expression.
Today's anti-smoking ads trump yesterday's smoking ads.
Flow of global youth commodity.

In words, structure of cars, ketchup, soap, shampoo.
Rock opera and some serious mayonnaise.
Resistance to right-wing marmalade.
Glowing in the disco light.
A final exercise in this novel routine.
Other advice on which games to play.
Industry filled with rocky road ice cream.
A missed opportunity or coma.
A symbolic button catalogue.
A financial exercise in this propeller.
A capital hungry to compete.

SOCIAL POSITIONS

A scale to measure
these cities and inconsistent
ascription.

A social fulcrum
wakes building
equality means abolition.

A small person wishes
in two senses
a bridge and a snowstorm.

A good meeting point
between lines
bottles a plaza.

A click is maximal
composition making meaning
contradict or play.

A notional idea of resistance
flows through homes
in electrical wires.

A sovereign virtue
precipitates slowly over
concrete societies.

A machine analogy
blinks lightbulbs overhead
triangles hold over water.

A ledge or bench
men watch the plaza
lift time or negate impostors.

A comforting ceiling
reserve army
proper appearance management.

A necktie associates
with penlights
click indicates.

A litmus trust
window forms
a paper plaza.

A play of residence
smiles writing
routine instigations outside.

A town or community
constitutions social capital
pulleys relationships between words.

A GENERAL ECONOMIC

All this fake math for productivity.
Minimize heat for lung injury. Oil leak
for goth pall. Stalin for food stamps.
Super babies for advertising fund. Sugar
for water. Thick wall for X-Ray specs.
Dance for dance. E.T. for Krypto. Phantasm
for schmantasm. Gawkers with butterfly nets
for white noise. Golden fleece for what to
catch? Animals drink clean water for
a panoramic ocean of nouns. Soccer moms
for taxidermy. Free rides for cash hoard
in river gut. Chocolate reform for fire
insurance. Flush toilets for blood pressure.
Home for airport. Rams grooved metal into
small porcelain neurons for people with
no jobs. Diet Coke and chocolate truffles
for commercial spam and a plastic sheet.
Like sweet cumswept determinant for water
is food-borne and fecal-oral. Atrophy a
damaged disk swathed in septic outflow
for to ravage with Photoshop. Windows open
at random for each table set with plates
and glasses. As all collaboration streamlines
new fragments into die cut vinyl more like
the tinny sounds a phone spews out between
two stations for procedure. Not a free gift for
machines blissfully move. Consensus for
catallaxy. Drug fixation for liver repair.
School and church music for cotton candy.
An icy crust covers all 'race incidents' for
purina feeds all physical attraction. A poem

that holds water for a poem that needs a catheter.
Anal fixation for arson. Contract pulls at
retina for movement over sound decision-making.
Eventually a vegetable for treats to double-wide
food. Yoga for pilates. A hot club for
a Freud vibe. Cute koalas for chocolate jets.
Varicose veins for product clangs from
the shank. In a plain brown wrapper for
dissolving grey matter. Chocolate chip waffles
and Chilean wine boxes for insurance. Oral
fixation for dry humping. On button for
committee. Direct democracy for iron lung.
Hammocks and so forth for knives sharpen
by drawing them. Inspections for pressure vessels
for showers with programming. Reinforce
support beams for hypochondriac. Surgery
for automotive grab bags. Gold clears
the table for trough coins through skin. Spent
face with talk for woodchips line the workplace.
New markets mark-up for pockets pick themselves.
Salted instead of Prozac for post-industrial
grindcore kissing noise. Terrorist talk is a
financial strain for ice-machine make-out session.
Music touches the alien ray for free sign up
but no obligation. Attach career to tranquilizers
for born in full blossom. Employment for
mosquito netting. Cool breeze for free fall.
Butterflies for discard. Investment in rhetoric
for painless echo. Rent for alms.

HE FELT LIKE A USEFUL LITTLE ENGINE

I come in for some criticism and
all I get is some hauling capacity.
I am a roaring column of gas and oil
like a plume of useful vehicles.

I dart behind my lids like a tendril
coaxes a sparkling clean mill into
a Rotax 912 or a suspended Passat
soaked in low-speed road irregularities.

Besides being a little tipsy, I grind
dry grains into my fuel tank. I crash
into a batter. I am a stairway
when pumping back drilling mud.

I descend at 225,000 feet and lean
with a twist-grip throttle. I feel sorry
for my unreliable voice. I swallow
like bounty does. I keep deep secrets.

LIFE IS SHORT, YOU'RE CAPABLE

Assume first that you're incapable
of tiring if you're a fan of first-person
shooters like mushiness or short

of breast feeding what sculpt a
butterfly or jumpstart a
car with personalized license

platter for your international
don't think you're capable of
loving any object without behaviour

when food could save
its battery life rather short compared
adolescent tantrum to toddler

caused by its "anti-noise
castrated writing microprocessor
capable of infinite reaction.

PEOPLE ARE SURPRISINGLY NON-VERBAL

Surprisingly, people don't turn up
as linear drawings of self, eg. 'my job
is a jail' or 'road, and have to avoid.'

Thump on the nose why dogs are
species making right hemisphere
acquaintance encoding cognition.

Bark bark talkers is easy bark gives
hand gesture a pound puppie snack bad
puppie chews on my sentence bad.

Introverts are easy to use lending
in library smacks lips together says
any paycheque nonsequitur keep job.

Stay out sign on a person's gaze back
to medieval age like, uh, 3, or neurotypical
honesty shouts at kennel behaviour.

ALL I ASK OF LIVING IS TO HAVE NO CHAINS ON ME

In a nearby room, I wish for a pinball
machine for it does make living together
easy, though you prefer to sleep.

Is it wrong to ask who will rule,
in the living room, with all that rocking –
t's crossed and i's dotted.

Better still, we issue a double CD,
with logos we can all display,
or how I comb my hair.

Brandishing a hyphen appeal,
even my parents bought into
the car parked there yesterday.

Do you own Victory, I mean,
if I tilt this game will you
ask me what I'm living for?

WE NEED HIGHER INFANT MORALITY RATES

First, we need conceptions of self
that delay speech, or rent regulations
that degrade quickly, thank you.

One of the points that need to be fed
is ointment on sinful diaper rash
baby bin high chance of cashback.

Attention, being male is a major risk
living in mud huts and higher income
ruts from hummer tires in suburbia.

We don't need less kids, just more
middle managers dyslexic and bonding
adolescent crazy glue cool, promise?

I AM NOT A VENDING MACHINE

I am now loyal to the company
because of pancakes at 3:00am.

I checked my head and this water
fountain just won't take change.

I want to watch my school burn down
needs a soda machine dispenser.

I am interested in vending machines
as a cure for all society's ills.

I am super pissed at 8:00 am
is curable by going cold turkey.

JOIN THE WRINKLE RESISTANCE

Grindaecology! Don't be a schmo!
Free small molecules in your slacks!

Join the linen revival! Carnival travel
pants! Or maybe, incromectant cramps!

Antistatic butyl rubber: it's free! Or
should be! Bob your pants on up!

Retire your iron! Freedom flat front
slacks! Inspect diet and lifestyle!

Easy-care sheets combine hot sex with
wheat! High performance fabric!

Yarn bulks up! All skin types quick dry!
Against your junk! Secret hiding pocket!

A FINE OCCUPATION

Wide enough for sleep, poems seek
a frugal material for quilting: feed sacks,
or pharmacy shelves. On the back porch,
a giant index of blues lyrics fetishized in
hymnbooks with lyrics halted, reupholstered,
appropriated. A scaled perestroika.
Globalization in deep harbours.

Yet even in winter, the paintings are beautiful,
landscapes with maple and birch with
rivers and frigates trampling seaweed. But,
is this a reactionary pastoralism? Self-
governance in period clothing? Leninism
won't preserve fabric – loincloths ooze
mule drawn plows, drudge, dirge, trees dig
new tributaries. Robots graze for apples.

During an auction, a fine arts education
cuts and sets gems, or waits
in a bank queue. Dissent is a fine point.
A net over fine hair. Is a fine occupation
useful, or is utility a fine occupation?

If classed work could exclude exploitation,
a consumer composes a fine compost.
Lamp is lit, poem is written, thermostat rises
with barely any social contract, just glucose
resistance, maybe diabetes. Leftovers
in the fridge: a taco, a stock portfolio,
a chest of gems, a hole in a sock.

In a union, two children are a form
of pastoralism. Shoals in the inner city
where a small hospital controls the coal trade,
Hydro-Quebec dams, schools where ancient
forests are priority fuels. Fast food
pressurized into sandstone or oil deposits.
It must be up to Mama Bear to broker a truce
among gangs, gas stations, home owners.

In a lamp lit cave, where binaries spread eagle
oratory in poor love poems, threshes in poplars
spin enough lyrics to fill an arts department.
But in ancient cultures, where any exchange
is within a system, the absence of a closed canopy
makes sword work of bristling formulas. First,
bang at nouns with verbs, then burst
into a room with words blazing. A linguistic
co-ordination of firefighting resource, but
since land ownership makes trade equitable,
capital's huffy aggravated sighing, matches
catalyst in an armistice like a candle. A fire.

Trees are tall; they care about the wildlife
that belongs. Work is routine, worthy of burning
at year end. Pastorals where wildlife owns
this line; underground railroad of the mind.
Each flower comes as a spray, a muscular
sweep toward centrism, or a ten-year apprenticeship
for neo-conservatism. Do commanders talk
straight or striate? Will an armistice end
an appetite for how atoms split or fast food cups
wagging arteries like a mace? A trowel? A constitution?

En garde against emoticons, agri-chemicals
contact antibiotic resistance. Pupils dilate;
things shine. A case for hallucinogens:
writing poetry. Yet dope makes dopey,
pulps beautiful urns. Tree resists horsehair
brush turn. Cut-up newsprint across the floor;
a single wharf boat drifts to wailing Hammond,
rock rock, in the body's sea. Fine linen, cilantro.
In a Marriot occupation, spores seize fine china.
Woolen socks wash in cool water, steam rise over trees.

Yet, isolationism children to death.
Ozone is a powerful anti-viral; asbestos
is conspicuous in the trachea.
Engineers hold their noses from the torch smoke.
Fishermen sit in gills and pull guts out,
a fine filet at The Keg, mint with the bill, where
a food-for-words program supplants work.

Syntax seeks a not candy, is produce if not
carnivalesque fast food. Traditional gab feeds
off tinder sticks that may light up faster yet
burn slower than books, even paperbacks.
Will come as a spray, these lamp-lit huts
in goosedown comfort. Genomes begin
catallaxing questions that replicate proper
genomes. If a book turns on subtitles,
stretching still photos to home video, then
lymph filters infection – paper is old, ink is old.

And in the dark, families graze like cattle, ideology
limited to canned tuna. Lichens form
closed mats. Quietists produce foodstuff.

Nearby, farmland is politicized. A fine-tuned machine prints banners that form a social-welfare state. A tangent of a smart business deal.

A SHORT HISTORY

My grampa shucked oysters in the war
risk free. Where do butterflies find
a piece of pipe cleaner and shape a
past from the fragments a roll generated?

The chance event most telemarketers
call a number at random. My grampa
devised a system for small libraries in
the war why leaves change in the fall.

A great science for people who eat
accountancy when numbers permute.
My grampa handled the anthrax mail
in the war to help or, at least, do no harm.

A PROMISING WORK

At the center for infections, I can get
the money I'm looking for. All this
making electricity gives me AIDS. I
tricked your germs into working.

If I had child care, would it be an exact
procedure? My disability cheque is a
promising body of work. Changing
work vouchers, I made my body into art.

My olfactory nerve is an envelope stuffing
kit. My joints crackle under the effort
of my home repair and loan scheme. In my
heart, a true vaccine is a pyramid scheme.

MY HEART SKIPPED A BEATING

I'm having an Oprah spasm.
How will the doctor
diagnose my arrhythmia?

Frequent diarrhea, aching muscles,
an article about beer;
progress stops then thuds.

Skips over my name at every
roll call, tired with more caffeine,
wires hook to spindly legs.

Budget-minded cyclical change
in the timing of a heart rate
vow I will repay.

How will a doctor
diagnose my business?
I slur breakfast operetta.

Touching the top of my stomach,
a stomach, or the stomach
a hand touches stomach.

EGG SALAD AND EXHAUST

I go to the cafeteria,
one of the food stalls
may have exhaust figures.

Blue shirts and potted exhaust,
junior high dinosaurs can
scrub the counters, mop the floor.

A shower of chicken salad.
My third Gravol roncos inside
my stomach sunny-side up.

Three minutes before searing
burnished leather scent
collects antique exhaust pipes.

On the move, the sidewalk defrosts
herring pieces, apple, onion.
Make me want to puke.

I'M AFRAID TO BE MYSELF

A big gush like I was uncontrollable
wetting myself in chocolate, instead
I always make sure I'm unsatisfied.

I didn't overindulge in waiting to have
a knife so I don't cut myself, instead
I stand on tall ladders and hug pillows.

I read repeating books all over myself
during the xmas holidays, instead
I was inconsolable over hugging myself.

I won't wait to have sex, trying to control
my illiterate chocolate cravings, instead
I eat myself, letting the poem repeat.

MY PANTS WON'T FIT

Damn sexy hamburger. Diabetes runs
in my hovel. My life is a belt.
Welts along my colon. I eat corporate.

Love handles taste funny. Food porn
social. Spills over pants in sexy
water damage. Cankle dance foundation.

Fat porn. Desexualizing the obese as
marginal. Lettuce is for losers. A norm
underlines form. Hot dog; ballet dancer.

Glossy fashion mags, yum. Paper has fibre.
I lied when I ate chips. Forgive me,
my stapled stomach leaks brake fluid.

A SPARROW'S SONG

Oh! A precious sparrow networks
with scarecrows of foil strips hung from
poplars; catwalks appear in the branches.
Our little sparrow plays games: Parcheesi,
cribbage; his heart dines on their seeds.
A snake that even hung a chickadee.

The sparrow shits upside down – ah! –
looking up at a yellow light, hangs up
his sword, tree and leaf, bird and bee.
Of cherry blossoms, eaves ease.
Beaver comes along, gnaws down trees.
A baby gift: fine motor, mother and father.

And, yawp, when moose eat sparrows, a nest
narrowly escapes a molesting antler. A molly-
coddling antitrust tests our hero's best
intent, incensed. Romance for the ladies. Darling
pirate shirt torn bears tufts upon tufts, swords
upon shards of stained glass. Cave is a hoard.

Now, a small concrete annex, a pool, wrought-iron
gate. Baby birds play. Traffic a carat. Scary
girders spout grass. Diamond a motel. L.A.
racing fake past celluloid ass. Love an
anagram, an anapest. A test of chivalry,
speed and synchronous teasing.

Ticket after ticket, show after show,
our sparrow nests in fitting places, fitting
row on row of patrons, chirping each a love

tune. Poorly fitting sheet metal, books are
overdue, polyvinyl nest in cavity dug
with Coke bottles. Hop on feet, twigs swell.

Keeping people's drinks topped is a clock
marking time on out our arms, peep peep.
A chirpy toddler leaps on the green,
bandages form garters hanging from
the candlewheel. A feel for harm:
meat is smoked to preserve it.

On the green, a sparrow leaps: mirror tiles,
orange peels. Two parts cream in this coffee.
In the coffers, love is a Wonder Bread truck,
a quick hump in a cab, pigeon tow liturgy.
Jump a homing signal, peep at self and
a sparrow peeps back, worm in beak.

For when film insiders nibble on ears,
seers skim Variety seeking scribes for
"The Maltese Sparrow", a dark noir.
Off the drink, our hero narrowly re-
cycles his ideas as, now, love is dumb
design software urban fuckscape skeeze.

But a nest, as whiskey stows crow eggs, kids
lay bids at daddy's feet. Work grows for
sparrows gorge on worms. Fat sparrows and
spy planes. James Bond and adhesive skids.
All romantic gullies swallow trash. Stink
of good ideas, progress, health and well-being.

Lesbia shares a malamar with her
sparrow – Catullus gets indignant and
swings a sparrow's song. Swipes
in a confederate tetris buiding project
for larks. Scores of wrong notes
along a cherrywood forklift love.

On the drink, gophers propose long poems.
It's analogy, wait, archetype makes sparrows
flee to alder or pine. A fund raiser, a croc nest.
Wordsworth weeps for poor arrows
splitting trees. On length, a mile is a good
as a pile; a gentleman as good as a dude.

Yet, monopoly, risk; Parker Bros. wake
the cave's alpha. Pop guns alert coolness
genes, no, jeans, wait, no jeans. Follow?
Fallow? Grizzlies desire fine suits to test
intelligence. Bubble sheets float soap to clean
eyes with epilepsy. Dice faint at ADD.

Bubble Bobble, bobble heads, bubble bath.
A good relax closets borders. Ancient sparrows
blow soap around ghosts. A pop, a bang.
Hula girl nests with twigs, plants row on row
of maize. Hold pencil against the wall, follow
string. Breadcrumb feeds lot. End stage math.

Here is Hansel mincing art. Shortbread
pinches nuke silo. Caramel drip painting, like
Pollock. A sparrow tips a forty for fairy tales.
A bat and a gatt. Shorty up in Pac's nest.
Sweet crib better to caramelize you with.

Shake your tailfeather, flap your ass.

In the labyrinth, Morgan Freeman's world
weary voice sirens soap actors to pen long
epics. Spectacle a cinch, feathers clipped,
horned or horny, skeeze an ever unfurled CG.
Worms on guard. Seeds pour from endless
sacks as mythril dips into burlap.

A sparrow with a twist: a remix. A sword and
a sideways cap. A spat over a piss off. A
lunch at mom's place. A kiss on the cheek.
A lip on a cup. A roll up the rim. A lovely
contest. A narrative closure. A sigh at the
end. A bending wooded path. A fork.

Yet, as Frost says, fuck choice, let freedom
race. Noice. Our sparrow lobs grenades at
glasnost – an 80's relic – instead it's Star Wars,
global spread of, and bottled coffee. Noise.
In Dolby or THX, hear nipples rub over
polyurethane, weather stripping over poise.

In the end, romance is easy, love a snap.
A sparrow cobbles a clean simulacrum with
tiny brushes made from thrush down. Mindful,
cavities burrow a lack, flowers suggest sneezes.
Sharing sugar water, bars upon bars, floor
as concrete, words as cottonmouth, mumbles.

SOCIAL PEDAGOGIES

At the heart of teaching
is a commons amalgamated
into suitable farming land. Slacks
and suspenders. Welding torch
is a suit to inspire grain. Sparks a
talked direction or digs trenches.
An aerator fork into soil, roots start
to breathe a private air.

A heartland, row on row of grain.
Water and sun, pesticide. A question:
close stalks outward like opposed magnets;
poles push then flip an arm's length.
Should a field push outward? In a race
where heart rate ought to increase
sneakers shovel dirt up.

The heart of a city is its road system,
how clocks keep time. An agenda;
an outline for research.
A fighting tree that needs no help.
An organic plan where signs are
spray paint; work crews for farming
activists. Commute is really nation
building in concrete matrix: desk on desk.
Is there a land claim? Question is attack;
a weeping-willow algebra
problematizes reflection's heart. To exist,
every dictator needs millions of jingoes
who never question. Answers are:
talking, chewing gum, making noise,

not, cheeks in roses. Instead,
a serious 7 year-old in his wool suit.

Here the heart is a water filter
that removes the large particles: bugs,
twigs. Sugar is refined in a mill. A student
asks about bug spray. Warning bell
answers that biodiversity is being lost.
Feathered coral feels it, sand banks sketch it,
teacher pleads with stalks to grow minus aerosol;
a plant less water grows regardless.

At the heart of local government is protest.
Stories of banks in the twigs
describe ancient science as magic. Poof,
there's alcohol. Waste paints and
paint thinner. Rational arguments include
no question that nature needs a commercial
to push clean water. Kids learn lists
contain inbuilt clocks taught to control
powerful neurochemicals.

Can the heart learn to choose
between material options? A Coke can
and a grizzly bear; a buick and
an ice cap; hey, my shoes and oh,
my soul. A dialectical Aesop might change
heart when he understands emptiness.
Students hold their injuries, look at the husk
and imagine it painted glittery trade.
Hannah needs puppets and Jon needs
change for the bus. Are moral lessons
absorbed through the roots? Homozygous,

designed to take each time. Damp soil
into the trenches for seedlings
or small trees, bonsai gently clipped.

The heart splits into four quadrants;
some students build roads, others build
banks. Farming, timber, coal.
Leisure time is essential, though,
in the magician's heart, demons are called
grasshoppers. Ants recognize a
moral obligation to build; they build terraces
on the slopes between parliament and
logpine to help cut and eat the first
tender stalks. No one could imagine
large classes in special buildings,
cool days of fall and never mature
before the first frost breaks open
the box built to hold.

Zoo directors go on a walking tour of the heart,
paint a convincing portrait of bars.
A narrative sickness counters an idea
of the world in question, tales of animals
who play the lottery each week
do not appeal to the commune for pay;
tales of animals who self-portrait
with brush strapped to head.

In the heart of the classroom, desks might move
into groups of four; bungalows into condos;
groups of picnic tables under poplar trees.
An outline for new kid programming
from market research applied next

to wadable streams. A glittery resumé
doesn't guarantee a better camera,
a clearer picture. Time to collaborate.
Governments and private armies,
smaller parties with hats and cake,
glittery star shiny and moral vacuums.
Groups for play and what. Here citizenship
is an object lesson on Hobbes. But coalition of
grassroots activism under fertile land,
not prairie, but mossy boreal.

Maybe the heart needs a plaza,
with Greek togas and Olympa-sized
torches. Is dialogue an exchange
of traffic lights? A messy business,
this heart: as if the key is all grow
in the same direction. Educators talk
of critical reflection; a student talks
about her Japanese heritage; local government
talks about globalization.

At the heart of this tale is mud,
razor-sharp grass; endless wonder
over rocks, clouds, ants, and warm cookies.
Teacher beats a drum loudly
until the paper head breaks. Windblown
deposits scatter over open spaces
in an enclosed area with an open fire
and could pollinate, multipliers,
bulbs stashed in their dens. Like magic,
social insects buzz around
heavy equipment to lift heavy verbs,
plant trees in lots, live in branches,
a common chlorophyll.

THE ECHO GAME

Destroy all textual source.

Bark Cartier second grade.

Cut raw meat tooth.

Embark powder spark work.

Fuzz all static wank.

Map all echo arcs.

Implode letter, knife wire.

Always fist tinny lip.

Hierarch suit shield ear.

Freshen saran logician puff.

Snag all linguist sweater.

Often cut meat art.

String oil baron mitten.

Shit faint pencil mark.

Bluster all head shake.

Brick foundation as boundary.

Erase typeface belt sander.

Raze name as machine.

Schiz cookie map lines.

Kill borders – magnet labour.

Truss carries – rush tallies.

Drop Stalin – Adopt Doughboy.

Book, chapter, paragraph, sentence.

Reset, rest; rest, reset.

Census, cents, sense, sex.

Defang echo – grind static.

Gape, gap; nape, nap.

Flesh bulge belt attack.

Rubble bust drug ring.

Each inside: circle, circle.

Black Sharpie – outsider art.

Egg just outside battery.

Birth shell anal desire.

Gaze, gauze, pause, pus.

Hands in the way.

Flyleaf, title, outrage, toilet.

Echo, echo; ergo, ergo.

Sounds like the better.

Echo, hole, lead, eddy.

Tuneless, toned, adstock, adhoc.

Absent, abcess, attend, atone.

Index, stridex, Ex-lax, flatulence.

Tree as precise order.

Rhizome as regal hierarchy.

A prairie flat echo.

Syntax a blossoming profanity.

Truly motivates; true motor.

And words shift constantly.

Elastic returns all ideas.

Unload text after text.

Discourse as high climb.

Canto engine pulls oil.

Machine noise pulls body.

Factory fills water bottle.

Paints a nice picture.

Brand, brand; and, and.

Suck slang through beats.

A voice-mail thought pattern.

Arcade question; I-Pod answer.

Nude beaches are sweet.

Video grope blue jean.

Apes, popes, pipes, smoke.

Reed, read; reel, real.

Bell, convention, reflex, echo.

Hauls, howls, cargo, jowel.

Rules, revolves, broken, anarch.

WATCH FOR EXPLODING CELLS

Exploding watches! Exploding pulsars!
Exploding pagers! Exploding Alzheimers!

Cell phone curdles my brain! Batteries
want wild action! Exploding aortas!

Brazil's exploding prisons! U.S. health
care staff craft fine chemical reactions!

I can hear my brain cells explode!
The exploding cells are sticky! Exploding

efficiency magnets, stifling explosions,
exploding peripheral explosions!

A new weapon in the war against explosions:
EXPLOSIONS! Hearing aids may explode!

I COULD JUST EAT YOU UP

Hello kitten, a smile like paint,
stickers still on paper, candy
bars then marshmallows, big
hearts, giardia then bathtime.

A shiny tarp, then a belly shirt.
Big eyes; garbage disposal. Bound
over mushrooms, sanrio turpentine,
perp, and then simple geometries.

Bitemarks, serum, then rooter.
Teeth, then Vespa. Engine, moon,
then pink. Fluff, then fuel. Out
of tune, then cute. Cut, then catsup.

SOME DEEP DARK SECRET

Dogface; dogfood. Rude; pooted.
Shelf; wealth. Leaf; leave. Escape;
cape. Superhero; stupor. Leak; liquor.

Poems are easy. Goatee comes off.
Cough as mask. Task as master. Bear
baits man. Breath baits metaphor.

Pinafore. Pirate flag. Stag film kills
fags. Straight as white. Civil, right?
Words can't stop. A rock in a face.

Language cracks nurture. Creature films
order. Beat on the other. Poem lacks
valve. Conscience fucks whatever.

SOCIAL UNDESIRABILITY

If I get slutty, will I still
heart bunnies and duckies.

Mom says black people are like
cavemen but they don't have clubs.

It's a baseball cap. It's a rapist.
I need to minstrel this shit up.

If you weren't so self-absorbent, I
could easily freek-a-leek with you.

The simulacrum of restraint is hey
shake your bum with your dumb.

Dad says homosexuals only like
to have sex with consumer electronics.

I talk, therefore, I have freedom.
No, alone. Help is a commie threat.

A plum choice between eats and pleats.
Voice is the stuff that comes from the mouth.

When we're at the store we try to be
efficient in how we follow dogma.

It's for my head injury. How the grinch
stole my virginity. More in an artistic way.

Teacher says retards are just like us,
except stupider and less important.

Maybe too pat and obvious when you
vacuum speech from the room.

English is hard. English makes a good
cold compress. English has many friends.

I will pull a glock on this shit if you
bitches don't respect my style choice.

It's where your brow sits that determines
your placement on achievement tests.

Neighbour says he is tired of drunk
indians always asking him for money.

Why buy new school pants? Instead,
you should buy new school overalls.

If the Chinese would just buy computers,
they'd solve their population problem.

Art is a controlled lack. Art is a sex
trade. Art is a lack of control.

I fell victim to victimization. It was hard
to avoid. Almost like a martyr complex.

Friend says that poor people should just
get jobs and they will be rich people.

I AM TIRED OF YOUR GAMES

Here is eating me alive for my close
friend and boyfriend want fries with that.

When people dogging my face I take
pills for taking stuff and some shit.

Because they think I'm fucked up
is leaving you – for good nobody.

That I'm bipolar and I don't want be
wit man scratch that never mind.

Since I'm through caring about fuck
and that's wait for you for ever.

GETTING DRUNK IS COOL

Hella woke up got lots of cool
pressies, chocolate and books, no
bad habits, just bad breath.

Drunk at random, I got crunked
at Dave's. I'm mad for Trish
drinking Carly. They rock my socks.

All the time morality, like some
illegal immigrants getting cool and
super funky. My arms are nice and big.

The coolest cool girl in the area
code for getting chicks drunk. Making
out drunk. I love his ears. No, I'm not.

MY PENIS HURTS WHEN I GLUE IT TO MY HAND

Stop! I glued my cock to my Coke.
I need sandpaper on my cock to make
fire. My CNN burns when I pee.

First, I pee some mo-ped exhaust, then
pull a gun made of shit. Hot coffee
hurts when it hits my dick. Sore to intense.

I boil my clothes, oink oink, my good
cock, spoink. Over the couch to knock
a chicken bucket away, a scavenger hunt.

Lastly, in the news, got a clue. Aloe Vera
gel or jump rope. A civil tongue in my ass
keeps my cock informed, infirmed.

BETWEEN COTTON AND CANDY

I hate cigarettes; I like boxes.
Fluffy grain dig botox crosswalk face.

I hate janitors; I like white bread.
Torrid argyle crapshoot candy floss.

I hate pants; I like requirement.
Cracker conduction polio aisle Volvo.

I hate bondage; I like Diet Coke.
Drunk custom vinyl hedonist candy apple.

I hate ethnic; I like orange drink.
Comp boot frosting opaque processed.

I'D RATHER HAVE A BOTTLE IN FRONT OF ME THAN A FRONTAL LOBOTOMY

As Groucho Marx asks, "Did he
dichotomy what guffaw?" with some
detergent. Cold here in the house –
need a tentoma or some cellade?

I'll listen to logic on CD, thanks.
On my PDA, I ate the right path
Frost mentions when he says, "Poot
nope over boots Dolly Patton, oops."

Down in the cellar, I might be dunked
but at least I'm not the Beijing zoo
where Pandas mumble, "weekend clean
dollar average insect bamboo, lunchtime!"

BECAUSE YOU'RE THE COMIC RELIEF

I like to polish my art. I want to part
with 3D stuff. My house is a ruin.

I'm a circus. I love difficult clowns.
My popcorn wants some butter.

I wasn't elected smart guy. I may be
heavier than dead. My mom said, "Duh."

I'm a magic word. I'm early because
the bus worked. My please beats turfs your thank you.

I'm involuntary. I want to hear reflexes.
My assassin brings me products I love.

ON LIKE DONKEY KONG

Like huge D-Pad buttons, a few
actually applied. Boss is so
barrel chested. My resume is
some shoot-em-up fun.

Like pop is carbon dated, I
get on a rhino and knock over
my fellow bowling pins. Boss says
I smack the right bongo moves.

Like Cabbage Patch fever all over,
nowhere but my corner office do I
break walls with my face. Boss says
Amazing Race is double length.

NO TALENT, ONLY TREND

Clang, clang. I wanna bang, Pavlov.
So talentless, you're laughing. Hott,
and getting spotted. Smokescreen
overcoat. Loads of alarm bells.

Denim, sputum. Booty call, booty
response. A logo on my crotch. Mime,
mime. My poem rhymes, Purdy.
Chocolate shots to the dome. Word.

Pattern, putter, plaid short pants. Golf
on a day off. Umbrella, coffee cake.
Milage to the limit. A laugh riot.
Bored, bored. I wanna hoard, Friedman.

MERITOCRACY OR BUST

Hey kids! Bid on high profile trades.
Own microbiology. Bankrupt chumps.
File bars under misc. Bust guns over
metro pop. Egalitarianism is a big word.

Stinks. Aces, Kings, Queens. Drink meat
juice for energy. Crush secular forces.
An organ without bodies. Slots tone calf
peaks and troughs. Unqualified is truly.

Clearly, push a button. Big box karate
schools. Electrical engineers are not stars.
Fuck while listening to the bottom line.
Touch bums in front of the mirror.

WHY ARE YOU LAUGHING?

Them apples asshole. Sale Viking
purple. Pressure intelligence agencies.
Giggle stalker sister. Solo race joke.

My mitten announcement. Minute
chiro pressure. Confucius stalks
vegetables. Sage stay disease.

Immune soloist bubble. Agency
drank praxis. Sick asshole joke. Wet
bolstering head. Lettuce race-car arms.

Viking justice mitten. Chiro revenge
bend. Redneck girl giggle. Bolster
immune pressure. Eat an apple.

THE DARK HEART

A hat and a carnival; conic freak; chronic sweatsuit;
black croc heel; even keel; ship at sea; rocking lion
jaw; Ibuprofen as law; green for marines; parrot mind
or carrot body; ellipse, ellipsis, elude, elide; slip
syphilis oil or fatty advil spectacle; glasses hold eyesight;
eyeliner slits perception; balls crib election; all the pink
competition; hands in eyelash shapes; whip makes grand
fire not on par with meritocracy; carbon paper catches
democratic fish; schools as wishful thought; ski mask
covers common sense; felt glued to the neck and
sticks glued to the hands and hands up the ass.

What this means is meritous parrotis. An honour, O knees,
if a rising tide lifts all boats, a canon lifts a poem that floats,
spectacle's rosy scent convinces theatre goers. Poem
explodes in spandex. Knockout gas mimics a horizon,
a trash bag, a cardigan, a legitimate democracy.

Yet the poem stands pollute, stumbles to the dark
heart of dark amidst a fleet of tin canoes, brilliant
sugar maples craft a landscape of wide-eyed chocolate
wrappers. Private sawdust soaks up crops. Orchards
vanish into picture books. Propellers vent family farms
into tight designer jeans. Landfills, rotation act,
industrial waste percussion, signification bottlenecks
brainwaves; work of all wordplay: codeplay.

Permanence a thing of the post. Trip out in the snow.
Only stone tablets fade. Tropes in folds. Painful
erection like a barcode. Rope holds back farm dog
from execution, carry out spectacle, maverick air,

aristrocracy. Bob Hope performs golf club poems.
Art moves for war with more fabric stitched in liquid
nitrogen, barns and farmhouses frozen. Close over
poems with quilts. Front face cereal boxes. Disposable
hot dog wrappers. Private face of public amnesia.

All this endless catallaxy, vintage college radio
kitsch wriggles an -ocracy on a line. Trophies for cute
smiles work hard enough, sand as white bent double
knock-knee spandex. Mute speaker sorts its own
compost. Constitutional legitimacy of the poem, when,
in the receding daydream, soundtrack is cream jeans,
capital cap tilts its brim; hats that merit wears.

What is socially ungraceful? Little lights flash how-to
vent, grrr, ohhh, arranging tiny flowers in current
box facades, or, maybe, ack, or arghhh. Meteors are
millionaires backward. A jewelled broach, a sash,
a weapon is lunch on a dim floor. Moths amass in poem
doors, pigeon holes which lower books. Pulp pulls up ink,
rounds up property and makes sharp news pages.
Tongue slips bees into the meeting to stir little petals,
but, stingers, meat won't bandage this tune, measured
with antennas, paper umbrellas, childhood opportunity.
Rain fire into a real fuck. "Bomb" on a placemat pokes cocoons.

In the pasture, dark at night, poverty with twister mats
builds a pulp mill. First, into the glass; second, into
the potato sacks. Picnic spectacle sings Appalachian
bluegrass out in old-fashioned nature flute muse on the way
to a vintage car rally. Scarf plays side of a face safety pins
punk rock pastoral smock. Art paints a scene. Gap gasps.
Dancing dismantles storms into an art. What is represent?

A falsely tuneful cool laid out in prairie flat?

First, man says to empire: beacon. Then, empire replies:
smallpox. Flicker in glass a coal mine cream in coffee
hardhat lamp up a receding scalp line. Swim to shore;
absorb noise. Confuse astronomy with oligarchy; god
with gawd; ass with moon. Teenage violence through
a widescreen Congo, or, maybe, shoot Haitians
in the face in Vice City. When Ezra Pound gets a
guest spot on 7th Heaven, will he wear a polo with cord
slacks. Bruckheimer flick ends in an act-off. Which poems
are courts? Which poems are gas stations?

Freedom is a hot fudge mudslide. Tape effect a real
disaster soundtrack spills a water bucket under the gate.
Title card spoons cake with fingers, rich like a dictator.
Paternalists in name only, Catherine Zeta-Jones remakes
Norma Rae in lipstick on Brad Pitt's collar.

Long staples sink into posts, securing wires to hold
the heart's growls, clearly repeats sing-song asap
shaking what into a discount bin an autoerotic ooze
through milk cartons or milf cartoons. Palms arched
over volvos mimic the billboard soup, a sound poem,
crisp, grunts out a new fifty with a ghost. Bird-calls
rattle seeds, plants need sunlight, models for life
shell skeletal fall leaves. Cosmet bemoans Walmart
miasma. Poem is a Kenmore nosejob. Grapefruit
for breakfast. Pockets sewn up tightly. Bed sores
coordinate with outfits. A game where art craves
soap and water. Wash in warm with like colours.

Carnivalesque health of land; heart stands fallow,
decompose, validation in trash typos as trash sorts
compost from sparrows. GM canola cuts bees
pollinating what birds eat. Art free trades however
it feels. If browse science makes choice democracy.
Camera echo exposed in liquid paper. Mystery stories;
multiple ambulances; SUV's; socially-conscious art;
period-costume sing-song; Aalzheimer's disease.

Gears chirp and chatter. Factory system shares
space with antique pistols, throwing knives, dunk tank.
A pulp mill compacts Elysian paper quality
into three stages: first, workers drain stock into
the Phong River, second, flows as frozen glass,
as sand rubs away a roll press. Plural of 'fray'.
Feet into pulp for trees into pulp for space. Third,
poverty; participle; zero effluent. China syndrome
a couple of typos. Collar on line two. Songs
on homemade instruments. Dark room where
photos develop raw colour. Poem cooks suspense
in a couple typos. Arrow points at product; to craft
instead of buy, raft instead of fly; to wait in line.

Democracy is as simple as a turn of phrase, dialogic,
right. Flicker in word-like LCD. Trees hide millionaires.
A renaissance fair; Tudor; weekday skivvies;
bowler hats; Zoloft; wicker chair; Oscar Wilde;
Calgary Sun; neoconhood; Robin Hood; dialing
for dollars; New Years Baby; Lotto 6-49;
Die Hard; Hamlet; Pokemon; Sistine Chapel; front yard.

FAKE MATH owes its existence to a number of things and people who have inspired and assisted this book on its way into the world. First and foremost, to the flarf collective, who gave me from afar a method and a perspective I sorely needed as I was trying to consider the purpose of my art in the world. Next, to the incredible support I have received from my fellow writers, teachers, and thinkers here in Calgary and beyond. Thanks to derek beaulieu, Christopher Blais, Christian Bök, Louis Cabri, Jason Christie, Carmen Derkson, Kevin McPherson Eckhoff, Chris Ewart, Alexandra Fidyk, Jon Paul Fiorentino, Aaron Giovannone, Jocelyn Grossé, Jill Hartman, Yvonne Hébert, Paul Kennett, Frances Kruk, Jani Krulc, Larissa Lai, Jeremy Leipert, Sandy Lam, Nicole Markotic, rob mclennan, tom muir, a. rawlings, Nikki Reimer, André Rodrigues, Andrea Ryer, Jordan Scott, William Neil Scott, Natalie Simpson, Fred Wah, Natalie Walschots, and Julia Williams. And finally, a special thanks to my family, who even came to hear me read, though, Mom, you may not want to read parts of this book.

The chapbooks *Social Commodities* (No. Press, 2005), *Adolesce* (above/ground press, 2005) and *Bad Shit!* (by the skin of me teeth press, 2007) contain sections and fragments of **FAKE MATH** in addition to publications in Avenue, dANDelion, fhole, Matrix, Nod, Originality of Orality Online, Peter F. Yacht Club, and Queen Street Quarterly. As well, work from this project has been featured in 2 anthologies: *Post-Prairie* (Talonbooks, 2005) and *Shift and Switch* (The Mercury Press, 2005).